I Have a Suicidal Student in My Office, Now What?

A Guide for Helping School Counselors Understand, Identify and Respond to Students At-Risk for Suicidal Behaviors

A School Counselor's Perspective

Dr. LaWanda N. Evans, LPC, NCC, CSC

Copyright © 2016 by Dr. LaWanda N. Evans

All rights reserved. No part of this publication may be reproduced, stored in a retrieval system, or transmitted by any means—electronic, mechanical, photographic (photocopying), recording, or otherwise—without prior permission in writing from the author.

To find out more about this book or the author, visit: www.drlne.com.

1106 S. Santa Fe Trail, #7
Duncanville, TX 75137

Cover Design © 2017 Christine Dupre

Disclaimer: The information provided is to be used as a resource, in addition to the policies and procedures your district has in place. You should not replace or substitute your district policies and procedures with the information provided, and the information should be used as a guide to help with students' emotional and mental health and educational planning only. I do not guarantee the success of any services or strategies provided. Schools, districts, school counselors, parents, students, etc. may choose to use the information to enhance their understanding, knowledge, and skills in the area of youth suicide prevention, or they may choose not to.

ISBN-13: 978-1541103658
ISBN-10: 1541103653
Printed in the USA

This book is dedicated to all school counselors, especially my school counselor friends in Grand Prairie Independent School District in Grand Prairie, Texas. Thanks for all you do for students.

TABLE OF CONTENTS

Introduction 7
Chapter 1: The Call I Will Never Forget 10
Chapter 2: Youth Suicide: An Epidemic 13
Chapter 3: Suicidal Behavior and Depression 17
Chapter 4: Some Facts About Youth Suicide 19
Chapter 5: Top Twenty Risk Factors 22
Chapter 6: Warning Signs 25
    Verbal Warning Signs 29
Chapter 7: School, Mental Health, and Home Behaviors 31
    School-Related Behaviors 32
    Mental-Health-Related Behaviors 32
    Home-Related Behaviors 33
Chapter 8: Prevention Strategies 35
Chapter 9: Taking Care of Yourself 42
Chapter 10: Resources 44
Tools You Can Use 47
    Screening Tool for School Counselors 49
    Due Diligence Checklist 55
    Script for Talking with Students 56
    Script for Talking with Parents 58
References 59
About the Author 62

INTRODUCTION

The purpose of this book is to help you understand, identify, and screen students at risk for suicidal behaviors. I'm a former school counselor with ten years of school counseling experience ranging from Pre-K to Early College. I received training from the American Association of Suicidology, and I was a School Suicide Prevention Specialist when I worked as a school counselor.

The topic of youth suicide prevention became very dear to me after losing a student to suicide in 2011; you will learn more about the story later in this book. Suicide is every school counselor's nightmare.

In this book, I will:

- Provide you with information on youth suicide prevention to help you become comfortable with talking to students and parents about suicide
- Provide you with resources and prevention strategies that I used personally when I was a school counselor
- Help you become confident in your skills and your abilities in working with students who are suicidal
- Provide you with resources and tools that you can have at your fingertips to help you in case you have a student who makes an outcry

On several occasions during my time as a school counselor, I felt the way you do now—scared and uncertain if the day would come when a student would walk in and say, "Yes," when I ask the question, "Are you thinking about hurting yourself?" I think this is every school counselor's nightmare: receiving your first suicide outcry by a student and panicking or second guessing if school counseling is really the path for you. Or even worse—leaving work feeling uncomfortable because you don't know if you did the right thing or handled the situation properly.

Well, I'm here to help you, guide you, and give you everything you need; but most importantly, I'm here to support you and provide you with the tools needed to effectively work with students, to decrease your uncertainties, to help you gain confidence, and to help you understand, identify, and screen students at risk for suicidal behaviors.

Hopefully, after reading this book, you will be confident in your skills and abilities as a school counselor in the area of suicide prevention, and you will become very comfortable talking to students, parents, and even teachers about youth suicide prevention.

Chapter 1

The Call I Will Never Forget

January 2011 was the month and year that changed my life forever. I received a call I thought I would never get while working as a school counselor—the one call every school counselor dreads, the one no school counselor wants to receive. The call that scares the world's best and most competent school counselor. The call that can take a school counselor to his or her breaking point. The call that changes the dynamic of a school environment from loud talking to silent whispers. Yes, the unbelievable—but so real—call that says, "We've had a student to commit suicide."

I remember the voice of my director as she spoke softly and

gave directions for the next morning in preparation for what we were going to face at school. I heard her, I was listening, but there was a part of me that was numb.

Once we finished talking, I was in a daze, and all I remember was dropping to my knees, tears rolling, and eventually crying out to God. I couldn't believe it—I wanted it to be a bad dream, and at some point, I would wake up from it. But it wasn't a bad dream. It was reality—a reality that has touched many families, friends, schools, churches, and communities: the reality of a completed suicide.

As I prepared for work the next morning, I remember thinking to myself, *This is going to be a tough morning and day*. I arrived at my school, but I soon had to go the school the student had attended to assist. When I arrived at the school, people were everywhere, and everyone was in panic mode and overdrive. We were all given a copy of her ID so we could know who she was, but of course, I already knew because I had seen her go through middle school and progress to high school.

As I walked through the halls, students were whispering and crying, sad and confused. I walked into the gym, and that's when it hit me all over again. I began to cry with former students who I'd seen progress through middle school and on to high school. Students who were impacted were all sent to the gym, where counselors and social workers were available to assist them as they grieved the loss of their friend and classmate.

Losing a student to suicide is an experience that cannot be explained or described. The emotions, the thoughts, the fear, the confusion, and—most importantly—the question that lingers in the minds of many: *Why?* This is a question no one can answer. It's a question that will forever go unanswered in the minds of those of us who have experienced the loss of a student, loved one, or friend to suicide.

Experiencing the loss of a student to suicide has a lasting impact, and it's something I will never forget. As a result of my experience, I'm motivated and committed to raising awareness about youth suicide, helping you identify warning signs and risk factors, and providing you with prevention strategies and resources to help you help students who are crying out for help.

CHAPTER 2

YOUTH SUICIDE: AN EPIDEMIC

Suicide touches the lives of many people, directly and indirectly, and has a lasting impact on the lives of those who have lost a loved one, friend, or student to suicide. This is a touchy subject for families, schools, churches, and the community, and many refuse to address the topic of suicide because of the fear of what may happen if it's talked about.

Each year, a million young people contemplate, plan, and sometimes attempt suicide, and every sixty-five seconds, a teenager attempts suicide. Suicide ranks as the third leading cause of death among young Americans ages fifteen to twenty-four, and in Texas, it is the second leading cause of death for fifteen-year-olds. Research shows that most adolescent suicides occur after school hours and in the teen's home. Every day, fourteen young people ages fifteen to twenty-four commit suicide, and approximately one suicide occurs every one hundred minutes.

Research has also shown that 27% of high school students have thought about suicide. 16% had a plan, and 8% have made an attempt. Females attempt suicide three times more often than males, but males *complete* suicide four times more often than females. 53% of young people who commit suicide abuse substances. Gay, lesbian, or bisexual youth have a two to three times greater risk of committing suicide than heterosexual youth. It is estimated that there are six survivors for every suicide attempt. Lastly, the Alcohol, Drug Abuse, and Mental Health Administration has declared suicide a mental health problem.[1]

As a school counselor, what can you do? How can you help decrease the number of students who attempt and commit suicide? This is a difficult and overwhelming task to take on, but it's not impossible. Some ways to help prevent suicide and decrease the number of students who commit and attempt suicide include:

- Everyone working together

---

[1] American Association of Suicidology. (2010). "Some facts about suicide." Washington, D.C.
Texas Suicide Prevention. www.texassuicideprevention.org.
The Alcohol, Drug Abuse and Mental Health Administration

- Being able to identify suicide risk factors and warning signs
- Screening students by asking the right questions
- Working with parents to identify protective factors
- Educating teachers and administrators on the signs and risk factors
- Teaching students the importance of asking each other, "Are you okay?" and reporting when a classmate or friend says no, can't answer, or if they have concerns
- Having suicide prevention training every year

Suicide is an increasing concern for schools and communities throughout the United States.[2] During the 1980s, there were an estimated 930,000 attempts for children and adolescents age ten to nineteen, and 10% to 14% of high school students reported that they had made at least one attempt.[3] As you can see, this is truly an epidemic, but by working together, understanding suicide risk factors and warning signs, identifying prevention strategies, and educating students, parents, and the community, we can help put a stop to suicide.

Suicide is a cry for help! Some youth have a difficult time dealing with issues and challenges in life. They face situations that are beyond their capacity to deal with and understand, and

---

[2] Capuzzi, & Gross, 2014
[3] Capuzzi, 1994

they feel as if they have little to no control over situations at home and at school. They feel like no one understands them and what they are going through. There are adolescents who feel like the world would be better if they weren't in it, and that's why it's important to recognize adolescent suicide risk factors.

Chapter 3

Suicidal Behavior and Depression

Two of the strongest correlates of suicidal behavior are stress and depression. Stress is any event in a person's life that forces the individual to adjust or adapt. Stress can be caused by a happy or sad event and even by having nothing exciting going on in life, which produces an unpleasant need to adjust to boredom. Stress puts a strain on an adolescent's life, and too many adjustments and difficult adaptations to various events in a short time can be an overload. No matter how happy or sad an event is, it requires an individual to adapt to change.

Depression is another strong factor that contributes to suicide attempts among adolescent students. Depression is a feeling that nothing is right. It is a psychologically learned response to the world and may be passed on from parents to children. Depression is shown in many ways, but in adolescents, masked depression is the most common. It usually comes out through restlessness, tantrums, fighting, sexually acting out, risk taking, and reckless behavior. Most of the time, adolescents show only the signs of masked depression.

Adolescents who are depressed may want to learn about the causes and treatments of depression to overcome this unpleasant condition, but when they are depressed, they often feel hopeless, isolated, and lonely. Therefore, they don't believe that anything or anyone can or will help them.

CHAPTER 4

SOME FACTS ABOUT YOUTH SUICIDE

It's important that you are aware of some of the facts about suicide, especially those that are important to your job as a school counselor to help become more knowledgeable and comfortable working with students who are at risk for suicidal behaviors. As I discuss each fact, think about the students you work with.

- Suicide ranks third as a cause of death among young people ages ten to twenty-four years old.[4]

---

[4] Center for Disease Control and Prevention and American Association of Suicidology, 2015.

- In Texas, suicide is the second leading cause of death for fifteen-year-olds.[5]
- More than one in every ten high school students reported having attempted suicide; nearly one in six students between the ages of twelve and seventeen have seriously considered it.[6]
- Females attempt suicide three times more often than males.[7]
- Males complete suicide four times more often than females.[8]
- Gay, lesbian, or bisexual youth have a two to three times greater risk of committing suicide than heterosexual youth.[9]
- 30% to 40% of persons who complete suicide have made a previous attempt.[10]

These are some alarming facts. Think about your students. If you're a high school counselor, think about the high school students that you're working with, and your elementary and middle school students. Think about the number of students who go home struggling with suicide ideation and actually go home and commit suicide, or even attempt suicide.

---

[5] TexasSuicidePrevention.org
[6] Youth Suicide Prevention Program
[7] American Foundation for Suicide Prevention
[8] American Foundation for Suicide Prevention
[9] Centers for Disease Control and Prevention
[10] Mental Health America

Think about the students you have in your school, how they're bullied or treated indifferently—even made fun of sometimes—while they're at school. This increases their risk of suicidal behaviors.

Sit for a moment and just think about the facts I just shared with you. Think about the students you work with every day. Any one of them could be included in those statistics. Now *that's* something to think about.

I know you're probably wondering, "She's only giving us a little bit at a time." Yes, I want to give you little by little by little because I don't want you to become overwhelmed. Suicide, or the discussion of suicide, is one of those topics that, in my opinion, shouldn't be given to you all at once. It should be given to you piece by piece to give you time to digest it, to really ponder and think about the information that's been given to you.

Chapter 5

Top Twenty Risk Factors

Risk factors are situations, circumstances, habits, or conditions that increase the likelihood of suicidal behaviors and thoughts, as well as suicide attempts or completion. Knowing risk factors is important because they help us pay more attention to the lives of young people and puts us in a position to ask questions when an adolescent exhibits questionable behaviors.

Here is a list of factors to look for to determine if your child or student is at risk for suicidal behaviors. Although I'm only providing what I call The Top Twenty Risk Factors, please note that there are *many* different factors, and adolescents may exhibit some of these factors and *not* be suicidal, but it is important to be aware, alert, and able to recognize some of the risk factors.

- ☐ Depression and/or feelings of hopelessness
- ☐ Sexual identity concerns
- ☐ Divorce
- ☐ Family and/or community violence
- ☐ Stress to perform and achieve
- ☐ Threat of AIDS or any physical illness that is chronic or terminal
- ☐ Loss of a significant person or other grief
- ☐ Break-up of a relationship
- ☐ Pregnancy/abortion
- ☐ Alcohol and drug abuse
- ☐ Distorted thinking patterns
- ☐ Negative self-talk or catastrophic thinking
- ☐ Sexual or physical assault
- ☐ Availability of lethal methods
- ☐ Family history
- ☐ Being exposed to suicide (school, friends, media reports)
- ☐ Impulsivity
- ☐ Psychological distress
- ☐ Perfectionism
- ☐ Poor coping skills and problem-solving skills

One of the risk factors I saw quite often was depression and/or feelings of hopelessness, which lead me to believe that when students are exposed to high levels of achievement and there is a lot of pressure to perform, their suicidal ideation is the highest.

Think about the students you work with. Are any of them at risk? Is there anyone you need to check on to make sure he or she is okay? Is there anyone you need to follow-up with because you know that there are some things going on in his or her home and you just want to check in? It's not to say that any of your students are suicidal, but you might want to check on them just to make sure they're okay.

Knowing what their risk factors are is important, but not as important as knowing the students who are actually at risk and the behaviors they exhibit. Knowing the risk factors will help you get to know your students better, and it will also aid you in creating different activities and programs to help meet their needs. It also provides you with an avenue where you can talk to educate their parents. It's important to have this discussion not only with the students, but with parents as well.

Chapter 6

Warning Signs

Youth who are suicidal want to live, but many of them struggle with emotional and mental health issues, abuse drugs or alcohol, have a very difficult time finding and seeing solutions to their problems, and find it hard to cope, manage, and deal with what they are going through. Under these circumstances, suicide sometimes becomes an option.

There are many behaviors and warning signs that tell us they are crying out for help, but sometimes it's hard to identify what they are because many of them are closely related to typical behaviors that young people exhibit while growing up. The following behaviors and warning signs below will help you identify if your child or student is at risk and help you become more aware. You may also visit www.youthsuicidewarningsigns.org for more information regarding youth suicide warning signs.

Warning signs are the out cries of a young person who wants help—that they want help and need help, but they're having a difficult time communicating that they need help. They're communicating to you, and to those around them, in a negative way when they're actually reaching out for help.

Being aware of the warning signs is very important; however, one of the best ways to know if a young person is suicidal is to ask. There's nothing wrong with asking, "Are you okay? Are you thinking about hurting or killing yourself? Are you suicidal?" I repeat, there's *nothing wrong* with asking those questions. Often, people think, *If I ask the question, then it's going to put it in their mind.* That's not true—you're asking because you are concerned. You're asking because you want them to get the help they need, and you also want to decrease the suicide ideation and the negative feelings they are experiencing.

The most important thing to know when it comes to warning signs is that it's important to determine whether or not the young person you're working with is, in fact, suicidal. Remember, the best way to know if a young person is suicidal is to *ask*.

Here are some warnings you may see when you're working with young people:

- ☐ Sense of hopelessness
- ☐ Feeling like there's no way out or feeling trapped
- ☐ Feelings of loneliness and isolation
- ☐ History of suicide attempts
- ☐ History of suicide in the family (especially on or around the anniversary of a suicide)
- ☐ Giving away valued possessions
- ☐ Planning one's funeral
- ☐ Poor adjustment to the death of a loved one
- ☐ Talk of suicide
- ☐ Preoccupation with death in writing or art
- ☐ Withdrawing from friends and family
- ☐ Low self-esteem
- ☐ Having no reason for living or no sense of purpose
- ☐ Loss of interest in and neglect of personal appearance
- ☐ Lack of interest in academics (decline in grades or failing classes)
- ☐ Dropping out of extra-curricular activities
- ☐ Noticeable weight gain or weight loss
- ☐ Insomnia or increased sleep
- ☐ Fatigue
- ☐ Self-injury behaviors or self-mutilation

- ☐ Increase in disciplinary actions
- ☐ Increased arguing with peers and adults
- ☐ Mood swings
- ☐ Negative change in peer group
- ☐ Vandalism, stealing, illegal actions
- ☐ Desire to or speaks of running away
- ☐ Suicide ideation
- ☐ Avoiding taking part in family activities
- ☐ Spending a lot of time alone in his or her room
- ☐ Being secretive about friends and activities
- ☐ Looking for ways to kill himself or herself
- ☐ Putting rubber bands around their wrist as a way to stop circulation
- ☐ Experimenting with what they call the "choking game"

In addition, a sudden, unexpected break from depression can be a sign. One day, they're depressed, and then all of a sudden, they say something like, "Oh, I'm not depressed anymore, so I don't need my medication." That's a really big warning sign there. Any expressions of hopelessness, worthlessness, powerlessness, or lack of control are also warning signs.

Those are the physical warning signs that you may see, but there are also verbal warning signs to look for.

Verbal Warning Signs

- ☐ "I'm so tired. I don't feel like I can take this any longer."
- ☐ "I don't want to be a bother anymore."
- ☐ "You won't be able to treat me like this much longer."
- ☐ "You won't be able to take it out on me much longer."
- ☐ "You'll be sorry."
- ☐ "I wish I wasn't here."
- ☐ "Life would be better if I wasn't here."
- ☐ "If I wasn't here, my parents wouldn't have to fight all the time."
- ☐ "I don't want to be here."
- ☐ "You'll be sorry that you said that to me."
- ☐ "Who cares if I'm dead?"
- ☐ "No one would miss me if I was dead."
- ☐ "What's the point of living?"
- ☐ "What's the point of living now that my girlfriend/boyfriend has broken up with me?"
- ☐ "What's the point of living? They don't like me anyway when I come to school."
- ☐ "What's the point of living? I'm always being bullied when I'm in school."

☐ "What's the point of living? The teachers don't understand me, my parents don't understand me, no one understands me."

Those are verbal warning signs that you may hear from students who are at risk for suicidal behaviors. Take some time and go through this list and think about some of those students who come into your office, some of the words that they use, and the behaviors that they exhibit that you see at school. If you feel any level of concern, consider calling them into your office to talk to them and make sure they're okay.

Chapter 7

School, Mental Health, and Home Behaviors

Students who are at risk for suicide exhibit many different types of behaviors at school and at home. These behaviors may place them at risk for suicide, suicide ideation, or even suicide intent.

You may see the following behaviors as a school counselor. Perhaps you haven't really given it any thought; but now that I'm raising awareness about youth suicide prevention, this is an alert for you to check on your students to see how they are doing.

School-Related Behaviors

- ☐ Tardiness
- ☐ Absenteeism
- ☐ Poor grades
- ☐ Truancy
- ☐ Low math or reading scores
- ☐ Failing one or more grades
- ☐ Rebellious attitude toward school authority
- ☐ Verbal and language deficiency
- ☐ Inability to tolerate structured activities
- ☐ Dropping out of school
- ☐ Aggressive behaviors or violence

Mental-Health-Related Behaviors

- ☐ Drug and alcohol use and abuse
- ☐ Eating disorder
- ☐ Gang membership
- ☐ Pregnancy
- ☐ Suicide or suicide ideation
- ☐ Depression
- ☐ Sexually acting out
- ☐ Aggression
- ☐ Withdrawal or isolation

- ☐ Low self-esteem
- ☐ School-related problems
- ☐ Family problems

HOME-RELATED BEHAVIORS

- ☐ Failing to obey rules or directives
- ☐ Avoiding taking part in family activities
- ☐ Spending a great deal of time alone in his or her room
- ☐ Being secretive about friends and activities
- ☐ Not communicating with parents and siblings
- ☐ Displaying values and attitudes different from family
- ☐ Resisting going to school or discussing school activities
- ☐ Arguing about everything
- ☐ Staying away from home as much as possible

Those behaviors may be common for some students, but for students who are at risk and students who may be considering suicide, these may be extreme behaviors, and they actually serve as an alert or red flag. This is to let you know that something may be wrong, that something may be going on, and that they may need help. These are behaviors you may see, behaviors teachers may tell you about, or behaviors that parents may tell you about. You may not see any of these behaviors, or you may see some of these behaviors.

This doesn't always mean that the student is thinking about suicide; but if you get a student in your office who may be exhibiting some of the behaviors or they are exhibiting some questioning behaviors, there's nothing wrong with asking the student if he or she is thinking about hurting himself or herself. In addition, it's okay to ask the student if he or she is thinking about suicide or have thought about suicide in the past.

CHAPTER 8

PREVENTION STRATEGIES

Suicide is preventable, and there is hope. The reason many adolescents commit suicide is because they lose hope. They believe suicide is the only way out and the best way to relieve themselves of their problems when, in fact, suicide is a long-term solution to a temporary problem. When someone commits suicide, everyone is affected and the problem doesn't go away. The only change that occurs when a person commits suicide is that they are no longer living.

As a school counselor, I'm sure you are swamped with so many things to do that you barely have time to effectively work with students who are suicidal or at risk for suicidal behaviors.

I definitely understand—I've been right where you are. The good thing is that you are not by yourself. You are not the only one who feels overwhelmed, tired, and frustrated, secretly wishing you had the necessary tools to help students, parents, staff, and the community by raising awareness about suicide prevention.

I have you covered! I've created a list of strategies—yes strategies, strategies, strategies—to help you. I understand that every school counselor loves strategies, and having them in place is important to your ability to meet the needs of students who are at risk for suicidal behaviors—not only students who are at risk, but every student in your school. It's important to always have a plan, to be proactive, and to always be prepared.

Here are some of the top strategies that I feel are very important, and are the same strategies I used when I was a school counselor:

- Raise Awareness in the School
- Provide Suicide Prevention Education—Staff, Students, and Parents
- Set-up Individual or group psychoeducational groups
- Refer to Community Agency or Mental Health Professional Counseling referral
- Collaborate with administrators

- Provide suicide prevention training for faculty and staff
- Create or be a part of the school-based Suicide Crisis Team
- Facilitate classroom presentations for students
- Provide suicide screening for students who are at risk
- Provide inpatient or outpatient referral information

One of the number-one strategies is to raise awareness by offering workshops and presentations for parents, students, staff, and the community. You can do this at PTA/PTO meetings, school board meetings, staff/faculty meetings, school-wide meetings, and classroom presentations for students, or you can offer a workshop on the weekend. If you don't feel comfortable speaking about suicide, bring somebody who is comfortable to come in and talk to your staff, students, and parents about youth suicide prevention. Not only do you want to raise awareness within the school and amongst teachers and staff, but you also want to raise awareness among parents. Think about speaking at the PTA meetings. Raise awareness by letting parents know some of the risk factors and what behaviors to look for at home.

In addition to raising awareness among parents and within the school community, you also want to raise awareness among the students by providing classroom guidance lessons on suicide prevention. You don't necessarily have to call it "suicide prevention;" you can call it "self-care for students." You can focus on coping with stress at school and at home. You can come up with unique ways to name your presentation so people can attend. There's nothing wrong with educating students about suicide prevention by providing classroom guidance lessons on suicide prevention. Actually, this is one of the number-one ways you can identify students who are actually at risk and be able to put a plan in place to help them cope with the issues and challenges that they're dealing with.

You will also want to do some type of group counseling. This is not to say that you're going to take all the students who are at risk for suicidal behaviors and put them in a group, but you may want to hold some type of ongoing group guidance lesson on coping skills. Remember what I told you in the beginning: students who exhibit suicidal behaviors, who attempt suicide, who commit suicide—it's a coping strategy. It's a way out. So, you, as a school counselor, have to go in and train students, give them the coping skills they need when they begin to feel overwhelmed, stressed, or as if nobody cares or nobody's there. Create some type of group guidance or group counseling lesson that centers around coping skills. You can call it whatever you want.

When I was a school counselor, I had one group called Panther Pals. I called it Panther Pals because that was the school's mascot, and the students were able to identify with the name. When they would come to the group, we would talk about coping skills, issues, challenges, and how to deal with different things as they come up. I also created a guidance group called Girls United, and created a whole curriculum for those girls, and the purpose was to teach them coping skills and coping strategies for life issues.

Every now and then, you'll need to provide outside counselling referrals to parents to help their students. Have a list of counselling referrals or agencies ready to be distributed to help parents, as well. Also, collaborating with your administrators is very important. Always let your administrators know what's going on, and don't ever keep anything that deals with suicide away from your administrators. Your administrators are your partners; they should work collaboratively with you. Always remember that somebody who is the head of the school needs to know when a student has made an outcry about suicide. I always tell school counselors, "Cover yourself." You have to cover yourself by all means necessary when it comes to suicide.

Create a campus crisis team. If there's no campus crisis team on your campus, then you want to create one. It could consist of the principal, the assistant principal, the nurse, you as the school counselor, and if there's another school counselor, the other school counselor. You want to have a parent on the team, if there's a parent that volunteers all the time. You may also want to have a teacher on the crisis team, and a student leader can be on that crisis team, as well.

Facilitate ongoing classroom presentations on a weekly basis. You should be going into the classroom weekly to provide guidance lessons to the students in your school. That's another good way to identify those students who are having a difficult time within the school environment and also at home.

If you're having a difficult time talking to your principal, try one of my favorite approaches. If there's a principal or assistant principal listening in, I always go to my principal or my assistant principal and say, "Hey, let me show you a way we can meet the social and emotional needs of the students in this school. These are the things that I've seen within the school. If I'm not able to provide classroom guidance on coping skills, dealing with life issues, handling stress, how to work better with others, conflict resolution, and anger management—if I'm not able to go in and provide guidance lessons to help the acting out behaviors and decrease the level of depression and stress that the students are exhibiting—if I can't do that, that puts our school and our students at risk for any type of inappropriate or dangerous behavior."

When I was a school counselor, I would sit and talk to my administrator about the importance of having classroom guidance. I would also bring data in to talk about and say, "This is what the research shows: that if we provide this, this is what will happen." You have to find a way to go in and talk to your administrators so that they can be on your side, so you all can work together, so you're able to go into the classrooms and provide classroom guidance.

Lastly, you need to make sure your district has some type of process for screening students who make an outcry. Now ask yourself, what are you going to do when a student comes to you and make an outcry? What happens when a student says, "I want to kill myself"? What happens when a student says, "I'm thinking about suicide"? What do you do? Do you freeze up? Do you drop everything? What do you do? Do you go home and think about it over the weekend and come back on Monday?

When a student comes to you, or if you're doing a classroom guidance activity and it's revealed that a student is suicidal, or has been suicidal, or is thinking about suicide, there should be a plan in place, you don't wait, you must respond IMMEDIATELY.

Chapter 9

Taking Care of Yourself

You work many hours taking care of students, especially students who struggle with suicide ideation, attempt suicide, or are at risk for suicidal behaviors. You spend a lot of time responding to the great demands of the job, working long hours, coming in early and on the weekends. But in the midst of everything you do, you have to take care of *you*. Taking care of yourself is very important, and you can't get so caught up in your job that you forget about yourself or your mental, emotional, and physical wellbeing. After you've met the needs of the students, you have to make time to meet your own needs, which includes self-care. I've gathered a list of things you can do:

- ☐ Laugh often
- ☐ Don't sweat the small stuff
- ☐ Ask for help when needed
- ☐ Know when you need a break and take it
- ☐ Leave work at work, and don't bring it home
- ☐ Eat well-balanced meals
- ☐ Exercise
- ☐ Get enough rest
- ☐ Acknowledge your fears
- ☐ Get a massage
- ☐ Spend time with friends and family
- ☐ Say "no" when your plate is full
- ☐ Allow others to help you
- ☐ Delegate responsibilities; you don't have to do everything
- ☐ Speak up when you become overwhelmed and stressed

CHAPTER 10

RESOURCES

- American Association of Suicidology
- American Foundation for Suicide Prevention (AFSP)
- Centers for Disease Control (CDC) Suicide Resources
- I Am Here Coalition
- Jason Foundation
- National Depressive and Manic-Depressive Association
- National Alliance on Mental Illness (NAMI)
- National Mental Health Association
- National Suicide Prevention Lifeline
- NIMH Suicide Research Consortium

- SA/VE (Suicide Awareness/Voices of Education)
- Suicide Prevention Advocacy Network (SPAN)
- SOS—Signs of Suicide Program
- Surgeon General's Call to Action to Prevent Suicide 1999
- Texas Suicide Prevention
- Crisis Line: 972-233-2233
- Suicide and Crisis Center of North Texas
- 1-800-SUICIDE (1-800-784-2433)
- National Suicide Prevention Lifeline: 1-800-273-TALK (8255)

TOOLS YOU CAN USE

SCREENING TOOL FOR SCHOOL COUNSELORS

I. Risk Factors—Check all that apply.

- ☐ History of prior suicide attempts
- ☐ Self-injurious behaviors (past or present)
- ☐ Feelings of hopelessness
- ☐ Impulsivity
- ☐ Anxiety
- ☐ Depression
- ☐ Drug or alcohol abuse
- ☐ Insomnia
- ☐ Family history of suicide or suicide attempts
- ☐ Mental illness or psychiatric disorder
- ☐ Loss of a relationship, finances, or health (real or anticipated)
- ☐ Ongoing medical illness
- ☐ Family conflict
- ☐ History of physical or sexual abuse
- ☐ Social isolation
- ☐ Work- or home-related stress
- ☐ Discharge from a psychiatric hospital
- ☐ Mental Health Provider or treatment change
- ☐ Access to firearms or lethal means

- ☐ Recently stopped taking meds without Doctor's knowledge or approval
- ☐ Lack of parental support or parent denial about suicide ideation
- ☐ Other risk factors: _____
- ☐ Other risk factors: _____
- ☐ Other risk factors: _____

II. Protective Factors—Complete each area.

- ☐ Ability to Cope with Stress: _____
  _____

- ☐ Religious/Community Connection or Involvement: ___
  _____

- ☐ Ability to Deal with Frustration and Tolerance: _____
  _____

- ☐ Responsibility to Others (Children, Family, Friends, Pets, Etc.): _____
  _____

- ☐ Positive Relationships: _____
  _____

- ☐ Positive Therapeutic Relationships: _____
  _____

- ☐ Support System (Family, Friends, Extended Family, Church, Community Resources, Etc.): _____
  _____

III. Questions to Ask Students

1. Do you have a plan? Yes or no? If no, move to the next question. If yes, describe your plan (if applicable).
2. What do you have access to in order to carry out your plan?
3. How long have you had suicidal thoughts?
4. What triggered those thoughts?
5. What has happened or changed in your life that has impacted you?
6. What type of changes have occurred in your life in the past three months? Past six months? Past year?
7. Have there been any deaths in the family, or have you had any recent losses?
8. Have you had a family member, friend, or coworker commit suicide?
9. Have you ever been treated for depression or anxiety?
10. Do you currently use drugs, have you used drugs in the past, or do you have a history of substance abuse?
11. Do you or a family member suffer from any type of mental health disorder (Schizophrenia, Bipolar, etc.)?
12. Do you have a history of attempted suicides?
13. Have you had any past or current fights with anyone?
14. What is your relationship like with your family and friends?

15. When was the last time you saw your primary care physician?
16. Why do you want to commit suicide? (Or, why do you want to harm yourself?)
17. Have you ever attempted suicide before? If so, when?
18. Describe what the world would be like without you.
19. Identify at least three to five people you are close to that you can confide in or that you trust.
20. Have you ever been in any type of in-patient or out-patient treatment?
21. Is there a family history of mental health problems or drug abuse?
22. Describe your relationship with your parents, siblings, family, etc.
23. Have you ever been abused sexually, physically, or emotionally?
24. Who are the most important people in your life?

IV. Risk Level[11]

☐ **Severe**—Suicidal thoughts, specific plan that is highly lethal, and states he or she will commit suicide.

---

[11] Substance Abuse and Mental Health Services Administration (SAMHSA), Suicide Assessment Five-Step Evaluation and Triage (SAFE-T), 2009.

☐ **High**—Suicidal thoughts, specific plan that is highly lethal, and states he or she will not commit suicide. Psychiatric diagnoses with severe symptoms, no protective factors, suicide attempt, and persistent ideation with strong intent or suicide rehearsal. States he or she may or may not commit suicide.

☐ **Moderate**—Suicidal thoughts with a plan, but no intent or behavior, risk factors with few protective factors. States he or she will not commit suicide.

☐ **Low**—Suicidal thoughts, but no plan, intent, or behavior. Modifiable risk factors (treated or controlled), strong protective factors. States he or she will not commit suicide.

V. Interventions—Check all that apply.

☐ Spoke with parents/legal guardian. Date: _____

☐ Met with parents/legal guardian. Date: _____

☐ Contacted Principal/Assistant Principal. Date: _____

☐ Contacted District Director. Date: _____

☐ Contacted Lead Counselor (if applicable). Date: _____

☐ Contacted District/Campus Social Worker or Nurse (if applicable). Date: _____

☐ Provided a list of referrals to the parents/legal guardian. Date: _____

☐ Made an inpatient/outpatient referral.

- ☐ Created a Crisis Plan/Safety Plan. Date: _____
- ☐ Implemented stress management strategies. Date: _____
- ☐ Provided emergency/crisis numbers. Date: _____
- ☐ Student was hospitalized.
- ☐ Taught relaxation techniques (deep breathing, imagery, muscle relaxation, etc.). Date: _____
- ☐ Recommended ASK App.
- ☐ Recommended counseling/psychotherapy.
- ☐ Provided psychiatrist/psychologist referral or follow-up. Date: _____
- ☐ Made referral for a full mental health evaluation.
- ☐ Provided crisis hotline numbers: 1-800-273-TALK (8255), 1-800-SUICIDE.
- ☐ Taught coping skills. Date: _____
- ☐ Encouraged journaling.
- ☐ Encouraged and discussed positive lifestyle changes.
- ☐ Encouraged and discussed exercising.
- ☐ Encouraged and discussed getting enough sleep and sunlight.
- ☐ Removed potential means to commit suicide (pills, firearms, knives, razors, etc.).
- ☐ Student received doctor-prescribed medication.
- ☐ Identified triggers and created plan to address them.
- ☐ Other interventions: _____
- ☐ Other interventions: _____
- ☐ Other interventions: _____

Due Diligence Checklist

- ☐ I've called the student to my office.
- ☐ I've completed the screening process.
- ☐ I have completed the checklists.
- ☐ I've informed the Principal/Assistant Principal.
- ☐ I've contacted the parents/legal guardian.
- ☐ The parent is meeting with me today.
- ☐ I met with the parent on _____.
- ☐ I provided the parent(s) with resources and referral information.
- ☐ I have read and explained the Parent Communication Notice to the parent(s).
- ☐ I did not leave the student alone.

Note: School counselors, *do not* leave a student alone if he or she has had previous thoughts or is thinking about suicide. Please call for assistance from your Co-Counselor, Counselor Assistant, Assistant Principal, Principal, or Secretary and have the student sit with an adult to be monitored until you're done talking to the parents. Use precautions.

SCRIPT FOR TALKING WITH STUDENTS

- Have you thought about hurting yourself?
- In the past week or two, have you thought about hurting yourself?
- Are you thinking about hurting yourself?
- If he or she says yes to any of these questions, say, I appreciate you for being honest with me. I know it was hard. Please describe your plan.
    - Do you have access to _____?
    - If you were to hurt yourself, how would you do it?
- Thanks again, I really appreciate you for being honest with me. It takes a brave person to open up and share such private information.
    - Remember when I explained confidentiality with you when we first met. Remember the reasons that would cause me to share information with your parents or other adults.
- Okay, great, I appreciate you for remembering. Before I call your parents, I want to first talk to you more.
    - Describe any loss you've had within the past six months.
    - Describe any changes that have occurred in your life that make you feel this way.

-
  - What do you do when you're stressed or overwhelmed?
  - Describe your relationship with your parents, friends, etc.
  - How do you handle failure?
  - What do you do when you are mad, angry, upset, or disappointed?
- Thanks so much, now let's talk about coping strategies.
  - Having thoughts of suicide or thoughts of hurting yourself are real. Here are some strategies and two cards I want you use when you have thoughts. Are you able to use this information? How can you use this information?
- Now, what I would like to do is call your parents to come to the school so we can talk together. First, I will talk to them by myself, and then I will bring you back into my office and you will have an opportunity to tell your parents how you feel. Is that okay?

Script for Talking with Parents

Create an environment where the parent feels comfortable.

Possible statements:

- Thanks for coming to speak with me about your child. I know it was hard to leave work, and I do apologize for calling you at work and asking you to leave early. But as I stated over the phone, this is an emergency, and I really wanted to talk to you face to face. Dropping what you were doing to come see me tells me you care a lot about your child.

- Remember when I discussed with you the limitations to confidentiality? Okay, great. This is one of those situations . . . [Begin to talk to the parent, put the parent at ease, and help the parent remain calm.]

- Now, I would like to bring your child back into the session so we can all talk. Are you okay with this? Are you ready?

REFERENCES

Berger, Kathleen Stassen. *The Developing Person Through the Life Span.* 4th ed. New York: Worth Publishers, 2004.

Capuzzi, Dave. *Suicide Prevention in the Schools: Guidelines for Middle and High School Settings.* Alexandria, VA: American Counseling Association, 1994.

Capuzzi, Dave and Douglas Gross. *Group Counseling.* 2nd ed. Denver, CO: Love, 1998.

Capuzzi, Dave and Douglas Gross. *Youth at Risk: A Prevention Resource for Counselors, Teachers, and Parents.* 6th ed. Alexandria, VA: American Counseling Association, 2014.

Davis, John M., and Jonathan Sandoval. *Suicidal Youth: School-Based Intervention and Prevention.* San Francisco:

Jossey-Bass, 1991.

Davison, Gerald C., and John M. Neale. *Abnormal Psychology*. 6th ed. New York: John Wiley & Sons, 2001.

Frankel, Bernard, and Rachel Kranz. *Straight Talk About Teenage Suicide*. New York: Facts on File, 1994.

Greene, B. and S. Uroff. "Quality education and at-risk students." *Journal of Reality Therapy* 10, no. 2 (1991): 3–11.

Hixson, J., and M. Tinzmann. *Who Are the "At-Risk" Students of the 1990s?* North Central Regional Educational Laboratory: Oak Brook, 1990.

Leenaars, A. and S. Wenckstern. *Suicide Prevention in Schools*. New York: Hemisphere, 1991.

Lewinshohn, P., P. Rohde, and J. Seeley. "Psychosocial risk factors for future adolescent suicide attempts." *Journal of Consulting and Clinical Psychology* 32, no. 2 (1994): 297–306.

Myrick, R. *Developmental Guidance and Counseling: A Practical Approach.* 3rd ed. Educational Media Corporation, 1997.

Parish, T. "Who are 'at-risk' and what can we do to help them?" *Journal of Reality* 15, no. 2 (1996): 90–99.

Parish, T. and J. Parish. "Validating a method to identify 'at-risk' students." *Journal of Reality Therapy* 12, no. 2 (1993): 65–68.

Rotheram-Borus, MJ, J. Piacentini, S. Miller, F. Graae, and D.

Castro-Blanco. "Brief cognitive-behavior treatment for adolescent suicide attempters and their families." *Journal of the American Academy of Child and Adolescent Psychiatry* 33, no. 4 (1994): 508–518.

Thompson, C. and L. Rudolph. *Counseling Children.* Pacific Grove, CA: Brooks/Cole, 1996.

Wilde, E., I. Kienhorst, R. Diekstra, and W. Wolter. "The specificity of psychological characteristic of adolescent suicide attempters." *Journal of the American Academy of Child and Adolescent Psychiatry* 32, no. 1 (1993): 51–60.

ABOUT THE AUTHOR

Dr. LaWanda N. Evans empowers and encourages women to love themselves, make healthy relationship decisions, and embrace positive changes in life that lead to happiness and improvement in their emotional and mental health. She has over fifteen years of experience combined working with elementary, middle, and high school students as a special education teacher and school counselor, and she has facilitated suicide prevention workshops for school counselors, teachers, parents, students, and mental health professionals.

She is a Licensed Professional Counselor; National Certified Counselor; Relationship and Life Strategist; Speaker; Contributing Expert Writer for *marriage.com*;

Advocate for Youth Suicide Prevention; owner of LNE Unlimited—Counseling and Emotional Wellness, LNE Unlimited Publishing, The Healthy Relationship Institute; and the creator of The Truth About Your Relationship.

Dr. Evans transforms the lives of women through counseling, coaching, speaking, and writing. She teaches singles and couples how to develop healthy dating relationships, healthy marriages, and healthy love.

Made in the USA
Middletown, DE
22 February 2018